SHOULD I MOVE?

A GUIDE TO SHELTERED AND RETIREMENT HOUSING IN SCOTLAND

CHRISTINE ANDERSON

AGE CONCERN SCOTLAND

Shelter
SCOTTISH CAMPAIGN FOR HOMELESS PEOPLE
21 YEARS OF SHELTER

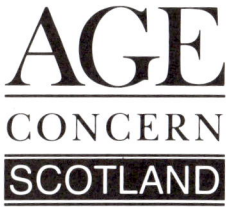

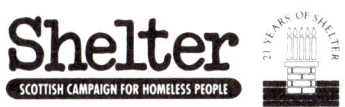

CONTENTS

Page No

INTRODUCTION	4
FIRST OF ALL - WHY ARE YOU THINKING ABOUT MOVING?	6
THE PROS AND CONS OF MOVING - THE ADVANTAGES OF SHELTERED OR RETIREMENT HOUSING	8
THE PROS AND CONS OF MOVING - THE ADVANTAGES OF STAYING PUT	10
WHAT POSSIBILITIES HAVE YOU EXPLORED TO HELP YOU STAY PUT?	12
YOU FEEL A MOVE IS THE ANSWER - WHAT ARE SOME OPTIONS?	22
WHAT IS SHELTERED AND VERY SHELTERED HOUSING?	27
SPECIAL CONSIDERATIONS BEFORE MOVING TO SHELTERED OR RETIREMENT HOUSING	30
QUESTIONNAIRE	36

	Page No
FINDING A SHELTERED OR RETIREMENT HOUSE TO RENT	40
WHAT ARE YOUR RIGHTS IF YOU RENT?	43
CAN YOU GET HELP TO PAY YOUR RENT AND SERVICE CHARGES?	48
FINDING A SHELTERED OR RETIREMENT HOUSE TO BUY	54
WHAT ARE YOUR RIGHTS IF YOU BUY?	56
CAN YOU GET HELP TO PAY YOUR MORTGAGE AND SERVICE CHARGES?	58
APPENDIX 1 CHECKLIST OF SCOTTISH OFFICE GUIDELINES	62
APPENDIX 2 PUBLICATIONS	66
APPENDIX 3 ADDRESSES	67
APPENDIX 4 BENEFIT RATES 1992/93	68

INTRODUCTION

Eight out of ten older people in Scotland may never need to consider moving.

Sheltered and retirement housing in Scotland has grown over the last 20 years and there are now nearly 30,000 such homes available either for rent or owner-occupation.

As the number has increased, Age Concern Scotland and Shelter (Scotland) have received an increasing number of enquiries for advice and information regarding this type of accommodation. This publication uses the questions most frequently asked in order that help with possible answers appears in a handy format.

The decision to move house is an important one at any time and at any age.

You could have many reasons for considering a move - you could have particular difficulties with your health; you could be physically or financially unable to manage your present home; you could feel lonely or isolated through bereavement or other circumstances; you could have friends or relatives already in sheltered or retirement housing who are urging you to join them or a new development could be being built locally which you can consider.

"Sheltered housing" or "retirement housing" are terms which conjure up an image of support and security in old age. The great majority of older people who make this choice consistently express a high degree of satisfaction with their new way of life.

It is, however, extremely important to try to consider all your options before you make any move. This applies whether you are considering renting or purchasing.

Remember, sheltered or retirement housing is an important and popular option, but it is not necessarily the only one. In fact, 8 out of every 10 older people in Scotland may never need to consider a move to any kind of supported home.

This publication covers the reasons why you may need to consider a move; arguments for and against moving; possible options; a definition of sheltered and retirement housing; who provides it; types of tenure and financial implications.

It also includes a questionnaire for you to fill in, based on your own circumstances, to help you with your decision.

FIRST OF ALL, WHY ARE YOU THINKING ABOUT MOVING?

Have you asked for advice from appropriate sources?

WHY HAS THE SUBJECT COME UP?

Can you take time to sit down and think through what it is that has made a move to another house seem a possibility? It cannot be stressed too much that you should never contemplate or undertake a move in a rush. Sometimes circumstances may seem so pressing that you feel action must be taken immediately. It is better, however, if you can make the time to consider alternatives and to ask for advice from appropriate sources if possible.

Simply finding the right combination of services or a source of extra companionship or activity or income may be what you need to enable you to stay in your own home.

WHO IS INVOLVED IN THE DECISION?

Do you live on your own at the moment or is the decision on whether or not to move one that has to be taken jointly by you and and someone else, for example, your husband or wife, other relative, friend or companion? If more than one person is involved in the decision, how far do you agree on the best course of action? If there is disagreement, how amicable is the discussion and will it be possible to reach a conclusion that harms no-one?

Is anyone exerting pressure on you to move and if so why? Will you have the support of family and friends no matter what you decide?

HAVE YOU RECENTLY SUFFERED A BEREAVEMENT?

The best advice that can be given to you in these circumstances is that you should try to avoid taking an irrevocable step immediately after a bereavement.

Remember that a move away from your present home, whether or not to sheltered or retirement housing, could mean a break with both people and places you love. Your present home will have many memories - memories that could help sustain you through a crisis. A rushed move could result in regrets at a later stage.

If you move immediately after a bereavement, you could also miss out on the companionship and support of some of the friends and neighbours who live around you now. Would you be able to visit each other easily if you moved and if not, how great a loss would not seeing them regularly be?

Try to give yourself some time to adjust to your new conditions and to work out your best option. You might like to contact an organisation such as Cruse which offers help to bereaved people. This could be advice on practical matters, someone to share thoughts and feelings with in confidence or the opportunity to contact other people in the same circumstances. Look in the telephone directory for the number of your nearest group or contact the address given in Appendix 3.

THE PROS AND CONS OF MOVING – THE ADVANTAGES OF SHELTERED OR RETIREMENT HOUSING

A MORE MANAGEABLE HOME

Are you finding that your home is now too large? Are there rooms that you rarely, if ever, use? A move to a sheltered or retirement house could provide you with a more manageable home providing warmth, safety and companionship and yet enable you to retain your independence. The aim of sheltered or retirement housing is to provide a living environment for older people that allows independence yet with support on hand as necessary.

CONVENIENTLY SITUATED

Modern sheltered or retirement houses tend to be compact, easily run units. Developers take great care over where the houses are situated so that it will be convenient for tenants and owners to

A sheltered house could provide companionship and independence

continue with all their usual activities. Most people go into a new development in an area they know so that links with people and places such as doctors and places of worship can be maintained.

AN ECONOMICAL HEATING SYSTEM

Your new house could provide you with a new and economical heating system. You would have the peace of mind of knowing that not only could you afford to have a warm home but that the surrounding passages and communal facilities were also always adequately heated.

HELP IN AN EMERGENCY

The presence of an alarm system and/or warden could give you greater feeling of security. It could also lessen the fears of friends and relatives who worry about you being able to cope on your own in an emergency even although you yourself might have no worries on that score.

THE STIMULUS OF CHANGE

A move could provide you with the stimulus of change. Not only the excitement of planning a move but also the impetus that new surroundings could give you to change your daily routine.

AN OPPORTUNITY TO EXTEND YOUR SOCIAL LIFE

You may find, for example, that in many developments where there is a communal lounge it is used a great deal as a focal point for their social life by the tenants or owners. You could also find that local leisure groups, which you can join, are allowed to hire the room for meetings. You could find the opportunity to take part in all manner of leisure activities close to your home without the worry of travel arrangements.

THE PROS AND CONS OF MOVING - THE ADVANTAGES OF STAYING PUT

IS SOME UPHEAVAL INEVITABLE?

The majority of older people who choose sheltered or retirement housing move to a development in a community they know. However not everyone can do so. Any move will cause a certain amount of upheaval in your life. If some or all of the following would have to change, and if they are very important to you, you would have to consider carefully whether or not to move at all.

DO YOU WANT TO LEAVE FAMILIAR SURROUNDINGS?

What are your feelings about your current home? When you look around it, is it important to you to remain in familiar surroundings where you can see concrete evidence of a happy life you want to remember? If you have been used all your life to a number of rooms in which to live and keep the accumulated possessions and

How would you cope with getting rid of treasured possessions?

mementos of a lifetime, would you be able to set about getting rid of items you no longer had the space to keep?

HOW MUCH SPACE DO YOU NEED?

How would you cope with living in a smaller home, perhaps only two rooms or even a bedsitter. How often do you have family or friends to stay? How big a part in your life do such visits play? Would you feel as happy providing hospitality if your visitors could not actually stay with you but had to fit in their visits when a development's guest bedroom was free?

WOULD YOU HAVE TO CHANGE ANY SERVICES OR FACILITIES YOU CURRENTLY USE?

How large a part in your life do people like your doctor, your home help, your chiropodist, your dentist or your health visitor play? How great a worry would having to leave any or all of them be? How would you feel if the distance you were moving meant that you had to find and deal with new faces?

Would you have to find a new place of worship? What difficulties would this make?

How about shopping and leisure pursuits? Would you still be able to go to the same places or would they all be entirely new?

WOULD YOU NEED TO MAKE ANY NEW TRANSPORT ARRANGEMENTS?

What are your current transport arrangements? Would you have to make new arrangements? Would you be able to do this without too much difficulty?

HOW WOULD YOU COPE WITH ANY UPHEAVAL?

You are the best judge of your own personality - how would you cope with the upheaval of the move, perhaps getting rid of treasured possessions, even pets, and having to make new friendships and new contacts? Would a move be a time of opportunities or would you find it contributing to your problems?

WHAT POSSIBILITIES HAVE YOU EXPLORED TO HELP YOU STAY PUT?

Are there ways you could summon help in an emergency?

COULD YOU GET HELP WITH A SPECIFIC HEALTH PROBLEM?

Has your present difficulty with your home arisen through either a sudden or a long-standing health problem? Are you unsure how long the problem will last or whether or not you can look forward to a full recovery? Does it seem likely you might have to go into hospital and are you uncertain how you would cope on discharge?

Or on a practical everyday level, are you finding that you have difficulty in doing personal things like getting in and out of bed, washing and dressing, going to the toilet? Do you need help with preparing and eating meals? Are you getting to the stage where you feel you really need someone around just in case you come to harm on your own?

If so, have you looked for advice and information on how community care is provided in your area? Have you asked your doctor, district nurse, health visitor or local social work department for information? They will be able to tell you about any extra help you can receive direct to your home.

Help could include having some or all meals delivered to your house. It could be having someone regularly each week who will do basic home help duties such as keeping your home clean and tidy and doing your shopping. Or it could be someone who will give you all the intensive help you might need round the clock for a short period, for example when you are just out of hospital.

The social work department or health services will also know about any respite care schemes available. Such a scheme allows you to make arrangements to stay in a residential care home, nursing home or hospital for a short period so that anyone who looks after you regularly can have a break.

They can also tell you about day centres and day hospitals where you could go on a number of days a week either just for the company and a prepared meal or to have something specific done that you can no longer do at home. For example some have special bathing facilities or physiotherapy and exercise sessions.

They also have information on aids that can be supplied to help you do things more easily yourself - things like walking frames or wheelchairs or even aids to help you put your clothes on or pull up your stockings or socks or turn taps or open tins.

WHAT WOULD MAKE YOUR HOME MORE MANAGEABLE?

How big a problem is your garden? Do you need help to keep it tidy and attractive? Do you worry that not coping with it affects yourself and your relations with your neighbours? Would you prefer to move to a house where most or all of the responsibility for gardening was undertaken by others or could you manage if you knew where to get help? Have you made any enquiries to see if there are any local schemes that could help with gardening?

Similarly with your windows. Do you have problems cleaning them? Do you have problems opening and closing them? Can you open and close your curtains easily? How difficult is it to take down your curtains for cleaning?

Have you asked if a home help would be able to undertake certain specific, heavier household tasks that you might need and could you perhaps pay for these services if necessary?

COULD YOU GET HELP TO COPE WITH LONELINESS?

Perhaps you feel lonely at times. You may have lost the love and companionship of someone dear. Your family may no longer live near you and costs and distance may mean few visits. As time goes on, your circle of friends may be diminishing. You may be finding that, through either lack of inclination or increasing disability, you are leaving the house less and less. Without realising what has happened to you, you could actually be suffering from depression.

Have you talked to anyone about your problem - your doctor, your home help, someone from your place of worship, someone from your local Age Concern group?

They may be able to put you in touch with local individuals or groups who are able to visit you or take you out when needed.

ARE THERE WAYS YOU COULD SUMMON HELP QUICKLY IN AN EMERGENCY?

Do you find yourself worrying about what would happen if you had an accident or suddenly fell ill at home? If you knew that you had the means to call help immediately in such a situation, would you feel that you could contemplate staying put?

If so, have you made any enquiries about having your home linked to a community alarm scheme? It is now possible for individual houses to be linked into schemes. Whether you are a tenant or an owner, if you feel you could take advantage of this, contact your local housing or social work department. They will be able to advise you if you could have your home attached to a local scheme and how much, if anything, it would cost. Knowing that you could quickly contact someone in an emergency might be all that you need to have the confidence to stay in your own home.

WHAT COULD YOU DO TO FEEL SAFER IN YOUR OWN HOME?

Are you perhaps frightened living on your own or does your feeling of insecurity come from the nature of the area you live in?

Would you feel safer with adequate door and window locks, a door chain and peep holes in your doors? Your local police station will be able to advise you on the best items and may even run or know of local schemes to help you install good quality fitments at a reasonable cost whether you are a tenant or owner. If you live in a property with a common stair you might be able to have a door entry system installed either by approaching your landlord or by coming to an agreement with other owners involved.

COULD YOU MAKE BETTER TRANSPORT ARRANGEMENTS?

Have you checked your entitlement to any local concessionary travel scheme? This could take the form of free or reduced travel on buses or trains or vouchers for taxis.

If you have to go regularly to hospital or to a doctor's surgery, you may find that there is a voluntary group in your area which has been set up specifically to help with such travel.

COULD YOUR HOME BE ADAPTED OR IMPROVED?

Are you finding that there are some aspects of your home that are beginning to cause problems?

For example, is your toilet easily accessible in relation to the rooms you use most? Are there stairs to climb either to enter your home or within it? Do you find going up and down them a problem now? Are they likely to become a problem?

Is your whole house heated during the day? Can you heat the areas you may use during the night - bedroom, hall and toilet for example. This is especially important if you regularly have to get up during the night for any reason.

Do you find that you have difficulty reaching up or in to cupboards? Do you have difficulty bending down to your electricity sockets? Can you manage to get in and out of the bath easily?

Whether you are a tenant or an owner, having work done to your home will cause a degree of disruption and perhaps mess. You are the one who must weigh up how vital the improvements are compared with how long it will take to have the work done and how fit you feel at coping with the possible disruption and mess. Would you have any worries over payment? Will not having the work done have an adverse effect on your daily life?

ADAPTATIONS

Whether you are a tenant or an owner, if you need an adaptation to your home to help you cope with a disability, first contact your Regional or Islands Council's local Social Work department, or speak to your doctor. Ask them to arrange for an occupational therapist to assess your home to find out what could be done to make it easier for you to use. You might then find, for example, that you could get help with the installation of a seat in the bath or grab rails above; a conversion to a shower; a ramp outside your door; a lift; central heating or telephone installation. Financial help is available from your District, Regional or Islands Council towards adaptations but as there is a limited amount of money available, you may have to pay some or all of the cost yourself depending on your needs and income.

REPAIRS AND IMPROVEMENTS FOR TENANTS

Does your home need some major repairs or improvements such as the replacement of kitchen or bathroom fitments, installation of central heating or insulation or rewiring? Does it suffer from dampness or condensation? Do you have problems with leaking roofs and gutters?

Have you checked to see if your home is due for improvement in the near future and if so do you know exactly what form the improvements will take? Do you have the option of paying yourself to have any improvements done sooner? If so is this something you could contemplate, for example by paying extra along with your rent?

REPAIRS AND IMPROVEMENTS FOR OWNERS

If you are an owner and you are faced with similar problems with your home, your local District or Islands Council will be able to advise you on the grants available for repairs and improvements and for conversion because of disability.

You may find that there is a Care and Repair service covering your area. Care and Repair supplies a project worker who will take owners through the whole grant process and find and supervise a competent builder for you. Schemes currently operate in Edinburgh, Aberdeen, Glasgow, Renfrew, Falkirk, Clydesdale, East Lothian, Western Isles, Applecross, Gairloch, Skye and Lochalsh, Nithsdale and Orkney. Other agencies throughout Scotland are currently considering setting up such projects.

In addition, the Edinburgh projects in Tollcross and Leith offer a small repairs service for the cost of the materials. Contacts for the projects are given in Appendix 3.

HAVE YOU CHECKED TO SEE IF YOU ARE RECEIVING EVERYTHING YOU ARE ENTITLED TO?

Whether you are a tenant or an owner, if you need extra money to keep up with the costs of daily living, you must explore every possible avenue of additional income you might be entitled to. You, or you and your partner, have probably spent your working life paying into the state system. If you need help now, claim what is yours - with the help of a local welfare rights worker or Citizen's Advice Bureau if necessary. You will also find the Age Concern publication "Your rights - a guide to money benefits for older people" extremely helpful (see Appendix 2).

Have you claimed everything you are entitled to?

HAVE YOU CHECKED YOUR BENEFITS?

Have you checked to see if you are entitled to any of the following?

- Basic Retirement Pension
- Additional Pension
- any graduated pension due on your own or a spouse's contribution
- Over 80's Pension
- Occupational Pension on your own or a spouse's contribution
- Widow's Payment
- Widow's Pension
- whether you could claim an increase for a dependant
- Income Support including the correct premiums
- Housing Benefit
- Community Charge Benefit
- Invalidity Benefit
- Severe Disablement Allowance
- Attendance Allowance
- Mobility Allowance
- Disability Living Allowance (from April 1992)
- Christmas Bonus
- Fuel payments in periods of very cold weather
- entitlement to free or reduced costs for hearing aids, chiropody services, prescriptions, dental care, eye tests and spectacles, hospital travel costs and items required for medical reasons such as elastic stockings, wigs and fabric supports.

If you are receiving a benefit, have you checked recently to see that you are actually receiving the correct amount?

If you discover that you have been receiving the wrong amount or that you have been entitled to benefit for some time but were unaware you could claim, make sure that you claim immediately. Ask for help from a local welfare rights worker or Citizens Advice Bureau, particularly if you are claiming backdated payments.

DO YOU HAVE A DISABILITY OF SOME KIND?

In April 1992, a new Disability Living Allowance will be introduced.

If you become unable to walk or virtually unable to walk before your 65th birthday, or if because of deafness or blindness you are unable to reach an intended destination out of doors without the help of another person, you should claim the Mobility component of the Disability Living Allowance. You must claim it before your 66th birthday otherwise you lose any entitlement. If you become severely disabled in some way, mentally or physically, before you reach 65, you should claim the Care component of the Disability Living Allowance. If you become severely disabled after you reach the age of 65 you should claim Attendance Allowance.

You should also check whether or not someone can claim Invalid Care Allowance for looking after you. This allowance can be claimed at the moment only by men under 65 and women under 60 who are unable to work full-time because they are caring for a severely disabled person for at least 35 hours per week. This distinction on the basis of age is currently being challenged in the European Court. It is therefore important that women between 60 and 64 who could claim this allowance do so now while the result of the European challenge is awaited.

If you are suffering from a disability because of the nature of your previous employment, remember that it may be worthwhile enquiring if you have the right to claim any kind of disability benefit and whether you can claim any backdated payments.

If you have any queries over entitlement, Age Concern's book "Your rights" mentioned earlier will give guidance as will a welfare rights worker or Citizens Advice Bureau.

COULD YOU RAISE MONEY ON THE VALUE OF YOUR HOME?

If you own your present home it may be possible to make use of the capital tied up in it through a home income plan or a home reversion scheme. Both of these schemes allow you to borrow money which is not paid back until the house is sold. If you wish to make use of your home in this way and you already receive a state benefit such as Income Support, Housing Benefit or Community Charge Benefit, it is important that you seek advice from a welfare rights worker or Citizen's Advice Bureau. This is because extra income or capital from such a scheme could affect your entitlement to state means-tested benefits.

If you do decide to use the capital in your home in this way, contact a number of companies to compare their offers before deciding which one you will finally accept. Age Concern Scotland publishes a free factsheet on the various schemes available (see Appendix 2). Remember to check the figures very carefully to see exactly how much money you will get in your hand each week as schemes involving interest charges will take away a substantial proportion of the loan.

HAVE YOU CHECKED THAT YOU ARE NOT PAYING TOO MUCH IN TAX?

Do you know exactly what your income is, how much of it is tax free, any tax allowances to which you may be entitled, the current tax rates and how to work out your tax bill?

If not, "Your taxes and savings - a guide for retired people" from Age Concern Scotland will help you check (see Appendix 2).

YOU FEEL A MOVE IS THE ANSWER - WHAT ARE SOME OPTIONS?

What are your options?

MOVING IN WITH RELATIVES

What about moving in with relatives? This might be a good solution but its success will depend very much on your relationship with your family. How well do you get on with them at the moment? Do you live for the moment they arrive but are you really quite relieved when they go and you can settle down by yourself again?

If you were to move in with them, is their house really big enough to allow you to have a reasonably separate household? Would you be able to invite your own friends to visit you as and when you pleased? If not, would it be because there was no room in which you could entertain separately or because you felt you should really ask permission while in someone else's home? Would this cause friction over time?

Would you be able to prepare and eat your meals and snacks on your own? Your reason for moving in with your relatives might be because you really didn't feel up to doing all of this anyway, but if this is what you would prefer how easily could you do it?

If you are quite fit at the moment, how would you get on in your family's home if you became frailer? Are there stairs, and how often would you have to use them each day?

What would the financial arrangements be at first? How easy would it be for you to perhaps question, change or disagree with them later on?

Is your family settled? Can you be sure that they themselves might not want to move at some later date for a reason that might not be connected to your living with them at all? How would you feel at the possibility of being uprooted again?

BUILDING ON TO A RELATIVE'S HOME

What about moving to a self-contained extension or flat built on to a relative's home?

This would enable you and your family to be together but live independently and might be the answer rather than moving in with them. Planning permission will be required from the District or Islands Council Planning and Building Control departments.

RELEASING A LOCAL AUTHORITY HOUSE

If you are a local authority tenant, perhaps living in a house that is now too big for you, Section 66 of the Housing (Scotland) Act 1988 allows a District or Islands Council to give you a grant to move out of that house. You must use the grant to buy a house or have an extension added to a relative's house.

You should check how the amount of the grant would compare with any discount you would be due if you chose to buy your local authority house. How far would the grant go in helping you to move elsewhere? Would it be enough to allow an extension to be built onto a relative's house? Would it supply sufficient capital to help you to buy another house? If there was any shortfall, how would you make it up?

A SMALLER HOUSE

What about moving to a smaller, perhaps newer, house with a modern central heating system, good quality insulation, small garden or no garden at all which you would find easier to cope with both physically and financially?

AN AMENITY HOUSE

What about moving to an amenity house? This can either be purpose built or an adaptation. If purpose built it will have the same design features as sheltered housing and will provide you with a good quality house without the care and support of a resident warden but perhaps with a 24 hour link to a central alarm system. Many local authorities have adapted existing houses to amenity standards, especially where large numbers of older people have been living in the same or neighbouring streets or in multi-storey blocks. Modernisation can include the installation of central heating, insulation and an alarm system.

WHEELCHAIR HOUSING

What about moving to "wheelchair" housing? This type of housing is provided by local authorities and some housing associations and is specially designed for disabled people, including older people, who have to use a wheelchair all the time. These houses have ramps and wider doors and corridors. Work-tops and electric sockets are at a convenient height. Disability Scotland (see Appendix 4) can give more information.

A MOBILE HOME

You could think about purchasing a mobile home. If so, remember to make extensive enquiries as to your rights to a pitch for your caravan on a site. Make sure you fully understand in what circumstances these pitch rights can be terminated or changed and by whom. Remember also that heating costs will be high, that you will be unlikely to find a site close to the amenities and facilities of a town and that such problems will increase if you become less fit. You may also find that you cannot sell your mobile home easily if you change your mind. Site owners may have the right to veto your sale if they do not like your intended purchaser.

SUPPORTED HOUSING

What about moving to a supported house of some kind? This could be set up in a larger dwelling with somewhere between seven and nine residents each having their own bed-sitting room which they furnish themselves. Each person can lead their own independent life but meets the other residents for the main meals of the day. These meals are prepared by a resident housekeeper.

The Abbeyfield Society is the main provider of this type of accommodation for older people - look in your local telephone directory for the address of the one nearest to you. Such homes are set up by interested local people who form a voluntary Abbeyfield Society in their area. They then look out for and convert suitable properties. They continue to take an interest in the well-being of the older, usually local people who come to live in the homes. Each house is financially self-supporting, with residents paying their own way. Charges (for full board) vary from house to house and help is available from the Department of Social Security or Housing Benefit for those on low incomes. Abbeyfield is a balance of privacy and companionship, security and independence for many older people.

NEIGHBOUR SUPPORTED HOUSING

What about moving to a home receiving neighbour support? This is where three or four frail older people are given individual tenancies, usually by a Housing Association, within an ordinary housing development owned by the Association. Four or five other people are then given individual tenancies within the same development and have a contract to provide the care needs of these frail tenants.

This form of housing is still very new and not widely available as yet. Edinvar Housing Association in Edinburgh has been the pioneer of this type of housing in Scotland. Contact the Scottish Federation of Housing Associations (see Appendix 4) for details of other Housing Association schemes.

RESIDENTIAL CARE HOMES

What about moving to a residential care home? These provide accommodation, meals and personal care. This includes help with getting in and out of bed, going to the toilet, washing, dressing and eating as well as help with laundry, shopping, taking medicines and housekeeping. Residential care homes are run by local authorities, voluntary organisations, housing associations and private proprietors. Both private and voluntary residential care homes have to meet standards for facilities and care, with local social work departments being responsible for registering the homes and for ensuring the standards are kept.

If you would like to know more about this option, a useful book is "Residential Care - is it for me?", available from Age Concern Scotland (see Appendix 2).

NURSING HOMES

What about moving to a nursing home? This would provide all the facilities of a residential care home plus full nursing care round the clock. Nursing homes are mostly run by charitable organisations or by private proprietors. Local health boards are responsible for their standards and for their registration.

If you find a suitable residential or nursing home, ask if it is possible for you to stay for a trial period so that you can consider if the atmosphere and facilities are right for you.

ARE ALL THE OPTIONS AVAILABLE?

This is quite a large range of potential housing for you to consider but your choice may be limited in a number of ways. Your state of health and the care you do or might need is obviously one thing to consider as is what you can afford. If you live in a rural area, you may find that some options are not provided locally as there are too few people living in one small town or village to make a communal development viable. You may also have difficulties if you have specific cultural needs.

WHAT IS SHELTERED AND VERY SHELTERED HOUSING?

What do you think the warden is there to do?

WHAT IS SHELTERED OR RETIREMENT HOUSING?

Sheltered or retirement housing is normally a development of purpose built or adapted housing with certain amenities.

A development could be a block or blocks of flats or it could consist of individual or linked bungalows. Some developments contain both. It will probably have been carefully sited either in the middle of an existing community or with good transport links, so that shops, health centres and leisure facilities are easily accessible.

An individual home within a development could consist of a bed-sitting room or have one or even two bedrooms and a separate sitting room. There may be a separate, well equipped kitchen or an area set aside where you could make light meals. You may be offered the choice of bath or shower or both.

There will be some form of emergency alarm system and/or warden service. Each home will be linked to an emergency alarm centre. In some developments, this alarm centre will be located within the development and the resident warden and their relief warden(s) will provide 24 hour cover themselves. In other developments the wardens will provide less than 24 hour cover. In these cases the individual alarms may be linked to a centre outwith the development when the warden is off duty so that the cover is maintained.

There may be other facilities available such as a communal lounge, laundry room and guest bedrooms with arrangements made for their heating, cleaning and maintenance.

WHAT IS EXTRA CARE OR VERY SHELTERED HOUSING?

You may find that, as the emphasis on "caring in the community" increases, you will have the option of considering a development that has been adapted or built to take care of people as they become frailer. These are called extra care homes or very sheltered housing.

In this type of setting, you would still have your own small house and extra help would be on hand for housework, personal care and making meals if necessary. Housing of this type can be available either within a sheltered or retirement housing development or as a unit on its own.

Many local authorities and housing associations are thinking about developing more of this type of housing for two main reasons.

One is that more and more people are living well into their eighties and nineties and can look forward to staying in a house of their own provided a degree of care is available. The other is that many current tenants in sheltered houses have been resident now for ten or twenty years since the developments opened. Some are now beginning to get a bit more frail. The adaptation to very sheltered housing will enable them to stay on in the house they know rather than move out to somewhere else.

In such a development, there may be a warden or "care co-ordinator" who has extra duties. This person may be involved in helping assess the amount of care a frailer person needs. They could also be in charge of home helps who work solely within the development and of kitchen and dining-room staff who help with meals for the frailer people.

As the private sheltered and retirement housing market is comparatively new in Scotland, extra care and very sheltered housing tends to be provided by local authorities and housing associations for rent at the moment.

SPECIAL CONSIDERATIONS BEFORE MOVING TO SHELTERED OR RETIREMENT HOUSING

Will living in a close community lead to stress?

HAVE YOU THOUGHT ABOUT HOW YOU WOULD COPE WITH A DEGREE OF COMMUNITY LIVING?

While living in your current home you can shut the door and have as little or as much involvement with the outside world as you wish or require. When you move into a sheltered or retirement house however, you are moving into a different environment.

Simply because of the way developments are built and managed, you will be faced with a degree of community living whether or not you decide to make use of any communal facilities.

So although it may seem harsh or irrelevant to suggest that you ask some of the following questions, you have to try to remember that living within what could be quite a close community could lead to stress of one kind or another.

Remember, however, that the vast majority of people who move to sheltered or retirement housing consider the move to be one of the best they have ever made.

HAVE YOU THOUGHT ABOUT WHAT HAVING A WARDEN MEANS?

What exactly do you think the warden is there to do for you? Do you realise that quite a few people have the wrong idea of what the warden's job is?

In ordinary sheltered or retirement housing, the warden is not there to do personal jobs like running messages, helping with your housework or keeping track of your medicines. Instead, as part of their caring role, the warden would try to ensure that any tenant or owner who needed help received that help from the appropriate authority. The warden is therefore someone that you could look to for help in organising any care you require rather than someone who would personally provide that care. The exception to this is when an emergency situation arises.

If you have any queries about the role of the warden, ask to see a copy of the warden's job description so that you know exactly what services you can expect. Remember that the warden has a very difficult job. It can be very easy for a caring warden, especially if he or she lives on the development, to work far more hours and do far more tasks than they are actually paid for.

WHAT WILL HAPPEN IF YOU MOVE TO A SHELTERED OR RETIREMENT HOUSE AND YOUR HEALTH THEN GETS WORSE?

You will have to think carefully about your own state of health and what you personally require by way of services before you consider moving. Are you thinking about sheltered housing as an alternative to residential care because you already suffer from particular problems? Or are you reasonably fit and see a sheltered or retirement house as the best way of preventing or combating any deterioration in your condition?

As you can imagine, the current and future state of health of the tenants or owners has implications for the warden's duties.

If a sheltered or retirement development has a high proportion of fit and active older people, then the warden will be in a better position to cope with the smaller number who have the greater need for services, while still being available to everyone as necessary. In this type of development you might find that, if your health deteriorated, you were expected to move somewhere else.

If, however, you were contemplating a development that had been built as very sheltered housing or if there were plans to convert it to that type of housing, then a higher level of warden support would probably be available to deal with a higher percentage of frailer people.

You should ask what would happen if your health deteriorated and you required more help. Would you be asked to move? How strongly would the request to move be put? Would you have any right of appeal and to whom?

These questions are important whether you are considering buying or renting.

If you are contemplating buying, read the section on the Deed of Conditions which will cover your rights in this situation. If you will be a tenant, your rights will be set out in your lease and you cannot be evicted or forced to move unless a sherriff agrees.

HOW WELL DO YOU COPE WITH ILLNESS IN OTHER PEOPLE?

One of the purposes of sheltered housing is to provide a way in which a community can care for some of its older, frailer, more vulnerable members.

Many developments are now being built or planned where there is a definite policy that a percentage of the homes will be allocated to frailer or disabled people.

Do you like the idea of living in a community that could have a high proportion of older or infirm people? Could you cope with perhaps being more regularly made aware of illnesses affecting people in your age group?

You may find that the communal lounge is used at certain times as a day care centre. It could be used in this way by both frailer tenants or owners and frailer older people from the community.

The use of communal facilities in this way is becoming more widespread as more and more people are living longer. In some sheltered housing developments, the partial change of use of an existing communal lounge to accommodate day care facilities is one of the first stages in the adaptation from a sheltered to a very sheltered development.

Depending on your own state of health, the availability or possibility of day care services could be just what you need to enable you to stay in a house of your own.

In addition to the lounge, other communal facilities may be available. A laundry with a heavy duty washing machine for example would allow you or your home help to cope with the regular washing required if incontinence is a problem. A bathroom with a hoist at the bath or seats under a shower means that you need have fewer worries about coping with increasing frailty as this kind of facility can be used by a health visitor or nurse to assist you with bathing if required.

If you are in poor health at the moment or know you are likely to be in the future, then such developments and facilities could be a positive reason for a move. You are the best judge of your needs and reactions.

Would you enjoy living in a community that was predominantly female?

HOW MUCH PRIVACY DO YOU REQUIRE?

How do you define privacy and how important is it to you? Would knowing that the warden had a key to your home make you feel more or less secure? Do you feel that the warden should only enter your home with your permission? How would you react if the warden knocked on your door and immediately entered without waiting for you to answer?

Suppose you chose a development where the policy was for the warden to use the alarm system for a "good neighbour" call to each home at some point during the day to check that all was well. Would you regard this as a welcome safeguard or would you see it as an invasion of your privacy?

Would you find it easy to discuss your preferences with your neighbours and warden and be assertive enough to insist on your wishes in any matter being respected or would you hide your feelings in order not to cause trouble?

You will know best how you react in different situations. You are the one who must decide whether or not a move to a sheltered or retirement house will or will not lead to stress in your life.

WOULD YOU FIND IT EASY TO LIVE IN A FAIRLY SMALL, CLOSE COMMUNITY?

Because of the differences in life expectancy of women and men there are likely to be three times as many women as men in sheltered housing. Would you enjoy living in a community that was predominantly female?

Sometimes, when people are living in a close community, it is easy for cliques to develop. If this had happened between some of the tenants or owners, is it something that would bother you? Would you feel perfectly able to cope with this problem if it arose?

HOW DO YOU FEEL ABOUT USING A COMMUNAL LOUNGE?

Is a communal lounge one of the attractions of the move? Would you expect to have an organised social life that revolved around the use of the lounge and be disappointed if either the lounge or the social life did not exist?

Would you see it as the chance to meet more people of your own age with similar tastes and needs or could it lead to stress if you felt you had to join in when you perhaps didn't want to.

You are the one who has to assess your preferred lifestyle.

HOW GREAT A SAY DO YOU WANT IN THE RUNNING OF YOUR DEVELOPMENT?

Research shows that only about one third of older people in sheltered or retirement housing really want to involve themselves in the running of their development even though the formation of a body such as a tenants' or owners' association can be helpful. Would you want to be involved?

How strongly do you feel that each person should have the freedom to make up her or his own mind on this matter. Do you think that those who do want to be active in keeping an eye on what is happening with the management of the development should be free to do so?

Do you want to keep an eye on what is happening?

QUESTIONNAIRE

Perhaps you might like to fill in the following questionnaire. Although there is no score to add up that will tell you whether or not to move, it sometimes helps to see your thoughts and feelings set out in this way when you have a lot to think about.

Tick the box that most accurately describes how you feel. There are some blank spaces which you can use to write in any items not covered that have a particular relevance in your circumstances.

PART 1.

Thinking about my personal and social relationships with other people and organisations -

	I couldn't consider a move if it meant losing contact with	Moving to the development I have in mind, I wouldn't lose contact with	A move wouldn't affect me as I don't have or would like a change of contact with
my immediate family			
my other relatives			
my friends			
my neighbours			
my doctor			
my home help			
my dentist			
my health visitor			

my district nurse			
my pet (s)			
my place of worship			
local organisations			
local clubs			
local shops			
others -			

PART 2.   My health

In the near future, I feel my health is -

Likely to improve	
Likely to stay the same	
Likely to get worse	

Thinking about my health and the help I need just now -

	I couldn't move as it would be impossible to do without help from	If I moved, I would still find it possible to get help from	I don't need/ expect to need help from
my immediate family			
my relatives			
my friends			
my neighbours			
my own doctor			
others			

PART 3.

Thinking about the overall quality of my life just now

	This means so much to me that I couldn't think of changing	This doesn't play a big part in my life just now	This is a problem I need to do something about soon
the comfort of my home			
the memories my home holds			
keeping all my personal possessions			
relaxing in my garden			
working in my garden			
my need for privacy			
my need for security			
transport arrangements			
others			

FINDING A SHELTERED OR RETIREMENT HOUSE TO RENT

WHO PROVIDES RENTED HOUSES?

Sheltered housing for rent is provided by District and Islands Councils, by New Town Development Corporations, by Scottish Homes (formerly the Scottish Special Housing Association) and by Housing Associations.

Housing Associations are non-profit making bodies run by voluntary committees with paid professional housing officers. Some specialise in housing for older people while others provide housing for many different groups. They take nominations from a local authority's waiting list and most have long waiting lists of their own.

TENANT'S HANDBOOK

When you rent you may be provided with a tenant's handbook which may give you information on a number of matters including information on any appeals procedure. While the tenant's handbook is useful, your legal rights are more important. These rights are set out in your lease and are covered later.

WAITING LISTS

It is important to realise that you could be faced with waiting for years rather than months for a tenancy in some areas.

SHARED OWNERSHIP

It is also possible to part rent and part buy a house. This is called shared ownership and is discussed later.

ALLOCATION POLICIES FOR THOSE WISHING TO RENT

By law District and Islands Councils, Scottish Homes, Development Corporations and registered Housing Associations must publish their allocation rules. Housing Associations must send copies of their rules to the District and Islands Councils in whose areas they have houses.

The law states that any rules must be available for you to look at, must be available for you to buy at a reasonable price and must be available to you in summary form on request.

Remember that waiting lists can be long and that different authorities and associations can have different priorities. The availability of sheltered houses also varies as older people do not usually move out of a sheltered house unless for extreme ill-health.

If you want to rent a sheltered house, you should approach the local housing office and ask to see the local rules on allocations. The rules may take into consideration any medical need to move, the state of repair of your current home, whether it is too large for your needs, whether you need to move closer to a relative or friend for care or companionship or their willingness or need to move nearer to you for similar reasons. Many landlords allocate houses according to a points system, awarding more points to those applicants with greater needs.

APPLYING FOR A DISTRICT OR ISLANDS COUNCIL SHELTERED HOUSE IN YOUR OWN AREA

Contact your local District or Islands Council housing office for an application form and ask to see their own rules on allocations, transfers and exchanges. Remember that you should also be able to see the rules of Housing Associations operating locally.

APPLYING FOR A NEW TOWN DEVELOPMENT CORPORATION OR SCOTTISH HOMES SHELTERED HOUSE IN YOUR OWN AREA

Contact your local area housing office for an application form and ask to see their rules.

APPLYING FOR A DISTRICT OR ISLANDS COUNCIL, NEW TOWN DEVELOPMENT CORPORATION OR SCOTTISH HOMES SHELTERED HOUSE IN ANOTHER AREA

Contact the main housing department of your chosen area for an application form.

You cannot be refused a council house in another district simply because you do not already live there - provided you are aged 60 or more and want to move to the district to be near a younger relative or else have special social or medical reasons for wanting to move there.

Your rights to go on a waiting list in another area are contained in the Housing (Scotland) Act 1987.

APPLYING FOR A SHELTERED HOUSE TO RENT FROM A HOUSING ASSOCIATION

Contact the Scottish Federation of Housing Associations for information on Housing Associations building in the areas you are interested in or send for Factsheet 8 "Moving Home - the Options" from Age Concern Scotland which lists those known to Age Concern Scotland.

Your own District or Islands Council housing department should also have copies of the rules of registered Housing Associations offering tenancies in its area.

CAN I APPLY IF I AM AN OWNER-OCCUPIER?

You cannot be refused a Council, New Town or Scottish Homes house simply because you are or have been an owner-occupier.

Your legal rights are set out in your lease.

WHAT ARE YOUR RIGHTS IF YOU RENT?

YOUR RIGHTS AS A TENANT OF A DISTRICT OR ISLANDS COUNCIL, SCOTTISH HOMES OR A NEW TOWN DEVELOPMENT CORPORATION

If you rent your sheltered house from one of the above landlords you will be a secure tenant. Most of your rights are contained in the Housing (Scotland) Act 1987.

RIGHT TO A WRITTEN LEASE

You must be given a written lease which describes the terms and conditions of your tenancy. Unless both tenant and landlord agree, these conditions cannot be changed except by a sheriff. No charge can be made for the lease.

NOTICE OF RENT INCREASES

As a secure tenant, you have the right to at least 4 weeks notice in writing if the landlord wishes to increase the rent.

PROTECTION AGAINST EVICTION

You also have protection against eviction. As a secure tenant, the landlord cannot evict you without first of all obtaining a court order. To obtain a court order the landlord would have to prove that there was a ground for eviction (such as rent arrears) and in many cases the landlord would also have to show that it was reasonable to evict you.

The landlord cannot take you to court without your knowledge and must notify you of the intention to take you to court. If you receive such notification contact a Shelter Housing Aid Centre, Citizen's Advice Bureau, local advice centre or a lawyer.

SUCCESSION RIGHTS

As a secure tenant, you also have some rights of succession to the property.

If you live in sheltered housing but the tenancy is only in the name of your spouse and that person dies you will normally have the right to take over the tenancy.

If you were both tenants (joint tenants) the surviving tenant will still have all the same rights in the house.

If there is not a spouse or joint tenant and the tenant dies, any member of the tenant's family who has been living in the house for at least 12 months will have the right to take over the tenancy.

If the landlord does not think that the new tenant needs sheltered housing then court action can be taken to evict the tenant. If this happens seek advice from a Shelter Housing Aid Centre, Citizen's Advice Bureau, local advice centre or lawyer.

A secure tenancy can only be succeeded to once. So if the present tenant succeeded to the tenancy and then dies, a spouse or family member cannot succeed and become the new tenant unless the landlord agrees.

REPAIRS

The landlord must keep your house wind and watertight and in good repair and must also keep in proper working order basins, sinks, baths, sanitary installations and installations supplying water, gas and electricity.

If you need a repair you should report this in writing to your landlord. If your landlord fails to carry out repairs you should seek advice as you may be able to take legal action to force the landlord to carry out repairs.

YOUR RIGHTS AS A TENANT OF A HOUSING ASSOCIATION

If you rent from a Housing Association your rights will depend on when you first rented from that Housing Association. The important date is 2nd January 1989.

HAVE YOU CONTINUALLY RENTED FROM THE SAME ASSOCIATION FROM BEFORE 2nd JANUARY 1989?

If you are the tenant of a Housing Association at the moment, and if you have continually rented from the same Housing Association from before 2nd January 1989, you are a secure tenant. This means you will enjoy all the same rights as other secure tenants. These rights are described above in the section dealing with tenants who rent from a District or Islands Council, Scottish Homes or New Town Development Corporation.

If the sheltered housing you are considering is provided by the same Housing Association as you currently rent from, you will continue to have these rights and the following additional rights in your new tenancy. If you have any doubts about this, seek advice from a Shelter Housing Aid Centre, Citizen's Advice Bureau, local advice centre or lawyer.

ADDITIONAL RIGHTS FOR SECURE TENANTS OF HOUSING ASSOCIATIONS

In addition to these rights, secure tenants of Housing Associations also have the right to have a fair rent registered. This is a rent figure which is set by a rent officer. The rent officer is an independent officer who sets a fair rent for the house. If the landlord or the tenant are unhappy with the rent officer's decision then either party can make an appeal to the Rent Assessment Committee. This is an independent committee which is normally made up of three people. The Rent Assessment Committee may confirm the rent set by the rent officer or may set a higher or lower rent. Once a fair rent has been set it cannot normally be changed for three years. A fair rent is the maximum that the Housing Association can charge for that property while there is a secure tenant.

HAS YOUR HOUSING ASSOCIATION TENANCY STARTED AFTER 2nd JANUARY 1989?

If your tenancy with a Housing Association first began after 2 January 1989 you are an assured tenant. If you now move to a sheltered house with the same Association you will remain an assured tenant.

If you are not already a Housing Association tenant and are moving to a Housing Association sheltered house you will be offered an assured tenancy or a short assured tenancy. Your rights will be contained in the Housing (Scotland) Act 1988 and are as follows:-

RIGHT TO A WRITTEN LEASE

You will have the right to a written lease. This means you must be given a written lease which describes the terms and conditions of the tenancy.

Although it is possible that these conditions can be changed without your agreement you do have the right to appeal any such changes to a Rent Assessment Committee.

RIGHT TO NEGOTIATE THE RENT

In assured tenancies the rent is "freely negotiated" between landlord and tenant. Assured tenants cannot have a fair rent registered.

Your tenancy agreement should if possible include a clause which states a method by which the rent can be changed and how any such change will be calculated.

If there is no such clause or if the landlord wishes to adjust the rent differently from that set out in the agreement, then a Statutory Assured Tenancy would have to be created by the landlord issuing a Notice to Quit. Within 12 months of creating a Statutory Assured Tenancy the landlord can serve a form which proposes a new rent (or any other new condition). If no agreement can be reached on the proposed change an application can be made to a Rent Assessment Committee who will then set a market rent. If your landlord wants to propose any changes then seek advice from a Shelter Housing Aid Centre, a Citizen's Advice Bureau, local advice centre or a lawyer.

PROTECTION AGAINST EVICTION

The landlord cannot evict you without first of all obtaining a court order. To obtain a court order the landlord must prove that there is a ground for your eviction. The landlord cannot take you to court without your knowledge and must give you a Notice to Quit and Notice of Proceedings as well as a summons to appear in court.

If you receive any such documents seek advice from a Shelter Housing Aid Centre, Citizen's Advice Bureau, local advice centre or lawyer.

RIGHTS OF SUCCESSION

When negotiating the conditions of the tenancy you can try to persuade your landlord to agree to allow members of your family to succeed to the tenancy if you should die.

If the tenancy is in the name of your husband or wife (or the person you are living with as husband or wife) and that tenant dies, you will have the right to remain in the house and become the tenant. This applies without the need for any special clause in your tenancy conditions.

You will not have this right if your husband or wife had already succeeded to the tenancy, but you could ask the landlord to agree to award you the tenancy.

REPAIR RIGHTS

Your landlord must keep your house wind and watertight and in good repair and must also keep in proper working order basins, sinks, baths, sanitary installations and installations supplying water, gas and electricity.

The landlord may also take responsibility for additional repairs and include these in the tenancy agreement.

If you need a repair you should report this in writing to your landlord. If the landlord fails to carry out repairs you should seek advice as you may be able to take legal action to force the landlord to carry out repairs.

RENTING FROM A PRIVATE LANDLORD

If you or your spouse first rented from a private landlord after 2nd January 1989, your rights will be the same as those who rent from a housing association for the first time after 2nd January 1989 (see above).

CAN YOU GET HELP TO PAY YOUR RENT AND SERVICE CHARGES?

HOUSING BENEFIT FOR TENANTS AND PART OWNERS

As a tenant, or as someone who part rents and part owns your home, you may qualify for Housing Benefit to help you pay your rent. (If you are the tenant and receive Income Support, your housing costs will be met in full).

Your rent includes charges for most communal services. This means that you can get Housing Benefit to cover your share of the cost of providing you with a warden, an emergency alarm system, any laundry room and equipment and the furnishing, heating, cleaning and maintenance of any communal parts of the development. Your share of the administration costs of providing these services can also be covered by Housing Benefit. These are the "eligible" service charges for Housing Benefit purposes.

HOW TO WORK OUT YOUR HOUSING BENEFIT

To be eligible for Housing Benefit, you must be responsible for paying rent and have no more than £16,000 capital.

To calculate the amount of Housing Benefit you will receive you have to compare what the law regards as your income with the notional figure the law considers you need to live on.

What you need to live on is called your "applicable amount". This is the amount of money that the government has decided is needed by people on a weekly basis, excluding housing costs, to keep them above the poverty level.

The amount is adjusted every year in April and is slightly higher for older people than for others. Details of the 1992/93 figures are given in Appendix 4 to help you work out your entitlement.

You must then work out exactly what will be regarded as your income. This is not as straightforward as it seems as some of the money you receive could be counted in full, some only partially counted and some could be disregarded completely.

The following pages will help you to do the two calculations for yourself.

COMPARING YOUR APPLICABLE AMOUNT AND YOUR INCOME TO SEE IF YOU CAN CLAIM HOUSING BENEFIT

If your income is the same or less than your applicable amount, you will normally get all your rent, including the eligible service charges, paid.

If your income is more than your applicable amount, your Housing Benefit will be reduced by 65p for every £1 you have above the applicable amount. This method of calculating the reduction is called a taper.

The maximum Housing Benefit you can get is 100% of your rent. The higher your income is, the lower your Housing Benefit. The minimum Housing Benefit payable is 50p a week.

If you think you might qualify for Housing Benefit you should apply. District and Islands councils deal with most claims for Housing Benefit although New Town tenants should apply to their own New Town Development Corporation and Scottish Homes tenants to their local Scottish Homes office.

The Age Concern publication "Your rights, a guide to money benefits for older people" is published annually after the annual uprating of benefits. This will help you work out your entitlement or you may like to consult a Citizen's Advice Bureau or welfare rights worker. See Appendix 2 for details.

WORKING OUT YOUR APPLICABLE AMOUNT

Your "applicable amount" is the amount, applying to you in your circumstances, that the Government says you need to live on.

You work this out by adding together the personal allowance for your age group plus the highest premium you are entitled to.

ADD TOGETHER:

THE PERSONAL ALLOWANCE FOR A SINGLE PERSON OVER 25

OR THE PERSONAL ALLOWANCE FOR A COUPLE OVER 25

PLUS EITHER:

THE PENSIONER PREMIUM FOR SOMEONE BETWEEN 60 AND 74

OR THE PENSIONER PREMIUM FOR A COUPLE WHERE BOTH ARE UNDER 75 AND ONE OR BOTH ARE OVER 60

OR THE ENHANCED PENSIONER PREMIUM FOR A SINGLE PERSON BETWEEN 75 AND 79

OR THE ENHANCED PENSIONER PREMIUM FOR A COUPLE WHERE BOTH ARE UNDER 80 AND ONE OR BOTH ARE OVER 75

OR THE HIGHER PENSIONER PREMIUM FOR SINGLE PERSON OVER 80

OR THE HIGHER PENSIONER PREMIUM FOR A COUPLE WHERE ONE IS OVER 80

OR THE HIGHER PENSIONER PREMIUM FOR A SINGLE PERSON BETWEEN 60 AND 79 RECEIVING ATTENDANCE ALLOWANCE, MOBILITY ALLOWANCE, SEVERE DISABLEMENT ALLOWANCE, INVALIDITY BENEFIT OR REGISTERED BLIND

OR THE HIGHER PENSIONER PREMIUM FOR A COUPLE WHERE ONE SATISFIES THE ABOVE DISABILITY CONDITIONS

OR THE CARER'S PREMIUM

The carer's premium is given to carers who are receiving Invalid Care Allowance. The conditions for receiving Invalid Care Allowance are quite complicated. Your claiming of the carer's premium could actually lead to the person you are caring for losing their severe disability premium which could be worth three to six times as much. You are therefore advised to seek advice from a Citizen's Advice Bureau or welfare rights worker or send to Age Concern Scotland for a copy of "Your Rights" before claiming this premium.

PLUS, IF YOU QUALIFY

A SEVERE DISABILITY PREMIUM FOR A SINGLE PERSON

OR A SEVERE DISABILITY PREMIUM FOR A COUPLE

You can claim the Severe Disability Premium if you receive Attendance Allowance and no-one is receiving Invalid Care Allowance for you. You must also be "living alone".

To be judged to be "living alone" the law says you do not necessarily have to live alone! You must be either single and living on your own or living with someone who also gets Attendance Allowance or living with a paid helper supplied by a charity. You could also be a joint tenant or owner and share housing costs. Or you could be one of a couple, provided you both receive Attendance Allowance and one of you has a carer who receives Invalid Care Allowance. The law is very complicated so you should seek advice.

You will receive a double premium if you are one of a couple, you both receive Attendance Allowance and neither of you has a carer receiving Invalid Care Allowance.

The narrow definition of "living alone" is currently being challenged, so if you think you may be entitled to this premium, make your claim meantime.

Contact Age Concern Scotland or your local Citizen's Advice Bureau or welfare rights worker to keep up with any changes to the law.

WORKING OUT YOUR INCOME

Any money you earn, any state benefits, occupational pensions and any other money you have coming in all count as income, after tax and national insurance contributions have been paid. The income of both partners is added together when calculating Housing Benefit for a couple.

DISREGARDED INCOME

There are some parts of your income that are not counted. These are called "disregards".

In your calculation ignore completely all Attendance Allowance or Mobility Allowance payments.

Ignore completely any actual interest or income you receive on savings or capital of under £16,000.

If you receive the special "pre-1973 widow" War Widow's Pension introduced in 1990, ignore this completely.

PARTIALLY DISREGARDED INCOME

Some further items are only partially disregarded.

If you are single and work, the first £5 of your earnings is disregarded (£15 if you are entitled to a Disability Premium or a Higher Pensioner Premium).

If you are one of a couple and either one or both of you work, the first £ 10 of your combined earnings is disregarded (as above, £ 15 if either of you is entitled to a Disability Premium or Higher Pensioner Premium).

The first £ 10 of any other War Widow's Pension or War Disablement Pension is also ignored.

District and Islands Councils are also allowed by law to implement more generous disregard schemes for those living in their areas who have been disabled or widowed by war. Unfortunately, not every authority decides to exercise the option but it is worth enquiring.

You are also allowed to ignore the first £ 10 of any payment you receive regularly from a relative, friend or charity but this disregard only applies so long as you do not also claim a £ 10 disregard for a war pension.

You must therefore look at all the benefits, pensions, earnings and other income that you have and work out how much should be disregarded.

HOW YOUR CAPITAL IS TREATED

You must then add on what is known as your notional or "tariff" income.

This is the income that you are assumed to be receiving from any capital that you have between £ 3,000 and £ 16,000. The actual interest that you may be getting on this capital is ignored. Any capital you have between £ 3,000 and £ 16,000 will therefore reduce your Housing Benefit on a sliding scale.

To work out this notional income, assume £ 1 of income for every £ 250 of capital you have over £ 3,000. For example, if your total capital is £ 3,001 it is assumed that the extra £ 1 over £ 3,000 will bring you in £ 1 each week in extra income. If your capital is £ 3,251, then that £ 251 is assumed to bring in £ 2 of extra income per week and so on.

This sliding scale means that if you have capital of £ 16,000 it is assumed to be producing a notional income of £ 42 per week . Neither Age Concern Scotland or Shelter (Scotland) is able to give you any information as to where you can find this kind of return on your investment in practice.

FINDING A SHELTERED OR RETIREMENT HOUSE TO BUY

WHERE WILL YOU FIND DETAILS OF SUITABLE PROPERTIES?

Consult local newspapers, solicitors or estate agents in the area of your choice. Some also produce free newsletters giving details of all types of property available. New developments for sale will be advertised regularly in such publications. You will also find "second hand" homes available.

WHAT IS THE DIFFERENCE BETWEEN "SHELTERED" AND "RETIREMENT" HOUSES?

In essence, there isn't one. Those selling properties often refer to "retirement" homes with a "resident manager" or "social secretary" rather than a "warden" but you are still buying a package which includes accommodation and service. You must therefore check carefully exactly what is on offer and the cost.

THE PURCHASER'S INFORMATION PACK

Whether you are buying a new or a second hand house, check to see that a Purchaser's Information Pack is available and how full the information in it is. It should give details about everyone involved in building and selling the house, the buyer's legal rights, consultation and complaints procedures, charges, services, the warden, the alarm system, repairs, insurance and procedure on re-selling the house.

DECIDING TO BUY

If you are buying a new house, check to see if you are being asked to put down a deposit on the property prior to signing an agreement to ensure it remains available while you make up your mind. If you are, how large is the deposit and will you get it back if you decide not to go ahead?

WHO ARE YOU BUYING FROM?

Check to see who it is you are buying your house from. The seller may be a builder who has done no more than build the house, a developer who both builds and manages the property, or a housing association or company that only manages properties. The relationship between all those involved in the building and managing of your house should be easily ascertainable and understandable. You must be able to see who you should approach if there are any problems and who has responsibility for what.

You will therefore need to find out the relationship between who is building and managing the accommodation and look closely at the agreement offered.

Don't sign till you understand and agree with the implications.

WHAT ARE YOUR RIGHTS IF YOU BUY?

THE NHBC CODE OF PRACTICE FOR PRIVATE SHELTERED OR RETIREMENT HOUSES IN SCOTLAND

The National House Builders Council Scotland is in the process of producing a Code of Practice covering new private sheltered or retirement houses. Copies of the Code can be had from NHBC Scotland (see Appendix 2).

Although the major developers in England and Wales have agreed to make the England and Wales Code retrospective, at the time of writing (March 1992) there is no sign of developers in Scotland agreeing to this course of action. The draft Scottish Code proposes, among other items, that owners should own their development completely, including all communal parts. It also proposes that, when the time comes for the appointment of the first factor of the development to be ratified, the owners should have a vote on that re-appointment. These two proposals have not enjoyed total support from developers of private sheltered and retirement housing in Scotland and it is possible that the code will eventually favour the developer's wishes where these two items are concerned.

You should therefore ask whoever is selling you a new sheltered or retirement house whether or not they will operate according to the draft code. If the answer is no, you will have to judge how important these two safeguards are to you — and to weigh up the urgency or necessity of your purchase.

If you are buying your sheltered or retirement house "second hand" from another older person, remember that they cannot grant you any extra rights themselves or make any promises on behalf of the current manager or original builder.

THE IMPORTANCE OF THE DEED OF CONDITIONS

While the law governing relationships between landlords and tenants gives tenants certain rights regardless of what is signed, the rights of owner-occupiers depends to a great extent on what is in the Deed of Conditions.

The Deed of Conditions contains a description of the property and services you are purchasing as well as details of the rights and obligations of purchaser, builder and manager and details of the procedure to be carried out in the event of a dispute.

When you sign your contract or otherwise agree to buy a sheltered or retirement house, you are stating that you have read and that you agree with the contents of the Deed of Conditions and that you agree to be bound by them.

Because of the importance of the Deed of Conditions, before signing any document to do with private sheltered or retirement housing you should consult a lawyer. Don't be afraid to ask your lawyer questions about any aspects you are uncertain of.

You should insist that you and your lawyer go through the Deed of Conditions, and any other documents to do with the proposed sale, clause by clause. This is to ensure that you agree with each and every clause before you decide to purchase. You should make sure that all the implications have been thoroughly explained to you, that you understand your commitments and that you agree fully with all the provisions.

Insist on taking the Deed of Conditions away to read over at your leisure if necessary. Under no circumstances should you feel pressurised to sign or agree to anything until you have fully understood and agree with the implications.

If you are thinking about buying a sheltered or retirement house you should therefore always get advice. Organisations such as Age Concern Scotland, Shelter (Scotland) and Citizens Advice Bureaux can give you general information. See Appendix 2 for details of publications.

CAN YOU GET HELP TO PAY YOUR MORTGAGE AND SERVICE CHARGES?

WILL YOU BE TRADING ACROSS OR DOWN AND NOT NEED A MORTGAGE?

Will you be able to consider buying without a mortgage? For example, you may have a house to sell. Ask if there is a part exchange scheme operating. This would mean less worry over selling your own home.

WILL YOU NEED A MORTGAGE?

You may be able to get an interest only loan from a building society. With this type of loan, no capital is paid back until the house is sold. You should contact a number of building societies to see which one will give you the best deal.

ARE YOU RECEIVING OR COULD YOU CLAIM INCOME SUPPORT?

If you receive or could claim Income Support you could have your mortgage interest paid. As the system is quite complicated, you should seek advice from your lawyer, local Citizen's Advice Bureau or welfare rights worker if you think you might qualify.

CAN YOU TAKE ADVANTAGE OF A DISCOUNT SCHEME?

Some builders and developers offer discounts or have arrangements with finance companies where a discount is offered on the purchase price. This is sometimes called a preferential purchase plan. You may be able to save up to 30% of the purchase price and pay nothing until you sell or leave the house.

Generally this means that when the house is sold you do not receive some or all of the increase in the value of the house. In some cases you might not even own the house but only have a life time right to stay there. The exact terms of such schemes need to be very carefully looked at.

WHAT ABOUT SHARED OWNERSHIP?

You could also be offered shared ownership. This is where you purchase a percentage of the equity in your new home and the builder or developer or manager remains the owner of the rest of the equity.

This allows you to keep more of your capital for living expenses. You might have the choice of later increasing or decreasing your equity share in line with your circumstances. On selling the property, your share in any profits will be equal to your percentage.

If you have savings of less than £ 16,000 you may be entitled to housing benefit on the proportion of the property that you rent. If you are unsure whether or not you would qualify ask a Citizen's Advice Bureau or welfare rights worker for help.

IS THERE A SCHEME AVAILABLE TO HELP YOU PAY THE SERVICE CHARGES?

If you take advantage of a shared ownership scheme and are entitled to Housing Benefit on the proportion that you rent you will currently be able to have all the eligible service charges paid. The section on Housing Benefit gives details of what charges are eligible.

You cannot get Housing Benefit to help pay for the cost of your home or the service charges if you are buying outright or if you are a co-owner. It may be possible, however, to enter an agreement with the builder or manager to help keep service charges down. You could agree in advance that a percentage of the resale price of your home will revert to the builder or manager of the development in return for lower service charges. If you have the option of such a scheme, make sure that you ask for all the details of the costs before signing anything.

CAN YOU AFFORD THE SERVICE CHARGES?

The importance of asking detailed questions about service charges cannot be over-emphasised. Most enquiries about private sheltered housing received by Age Concern Scotland are about service charges.

You must consider your financial situation extremely carefully. After you have calculated the initial capital costs and any ongoing mortgage costs, you MUST look carefully at your remaining income. Although you will probably be buying a modern home and can expect quite competitive running costs for fuel, there are likely to be few substantial changes to your other household costs.

At current costs, you will probably have to set aside between £60 and £100 a month for service charges. This means that you will either have to have an income or pension that will cope with that or have capital that you can invest for the sole purpose of paying these charges.

You should ask the following questions. How much will the service charge be? What does it cover? Can you afford it? How is it calculated initially? How low is the first year's service charge compared to other developments? Is this artificially low to encourage purchase? How often must it be paid? How is it to be reviewed and increased? Is there a consultation process before any increases? How much note does the manager or factor have to take of your views and the views of other owners when proposing or setting the charge?

Remember to consider not only whether you can cope with the service charge just now, but whether you will be able to cope with it in the future.

WHAT DOES THE SERVICE CHARGE COVER?

Normally the service charge will cover warden services. You need to look at exactly what is being provided by the warden. Ask to see a job description. Make sure that you fully understand any arrangements that will be made for the warden to have time off and what alternative arrangements are made at those times.

Check that the service charge also covers the following: communal cleaning and maintenance of communal gardens and other communal areas; maintenance contracts for communal amenities (alarms, lifts etc); maintenance of the building itself and repairs to it; insurance for the buildings. Service charges will not cover your own household contents insurance.

If the development you are thinking of buying into has been in operation for a while, or if the management company has been responsible for the management of other schemes, ask what increases in service charges there have been.

You should be particularly careful about repairing obligations and ensure that you get a clear statement on who is responsible for what.

If major repairs are needed, ask if this cost is already anticipated as part of the service charge. How much of the service charge is put into a special fund for major repairs? In some cases contingency or "sinking fund" payments for major repairs will be due when the property is resold rather than being included in the ongoing service charge. If this is the case you should look closely at exactly what will be charged.

FUTURE COSTS OR DEDUCTIONS

You should also ask about future costs or deductions. Will a charge be made when the property is resold? Can you sell to anyone you like provided they are a certain age or do you need the agreement of the management company?

Can you get help with your mortgage and service charges?

APPENDIX 1
CHECKLIST OF SCOTTISH OFFICE GUIDELINES FOR SHELTERED HOUSING

The recommended standards for sheltered homes cover a great many areas, some regarded as essential and some being optional. Only local authority and housing association houses HAVE TO COMPLY with the Scottish Office guidelines on standards for sheltered homes for older people - others may do. Whether renting or buying study a development carefully to see exactly what is on offer.

ESSENTIAL FEATURES TO LOOK FOR ACCORDING TO SCOTTISH OFFICE GUIDELINES

OUTSIDE

The preferred option is for a house at ground or first floor level. If the development is over two storeys high, look for at least one lift in each block. If there are more than 12 homes above the fourth floor, two lifts must be provided.

There will be a house provided for the warden either within the development or nearby. If it is a larger development that you are looking at, you might find that an extra warden's house has been provided.

You are unlikely to find that garages for cars are available. According to the guidelines, the warden is the only one who should have a car parking space. The minimum spaces supplied for residents need be only one in four. Many developments will have over this minimum, but if you are a car owner, be careful to check the availability of a space for yourself and what it costs.

COMMUNAL AREAS

Within a development, there will be a number of stairs, passages and open areas that are for everyone's use. In these communal parts, look for handrails on both sides of all stairs and on at least one side of all access areas and passages.

WITHIN AN APARTMENT

In the bathroom, the doors should either slide backwards and forwards or be the type that open outwards into a bedroom, living room or passage. This is so that someone on the outside could open them easily if you had fallen in the bathroom and were blocking the door. You should also be able to open any locks on bathroom doors from the outside.

Look for non-slip floors in all bathrooms and handholds fixed beside both the bath or shower and the toilet.

Ask questions about the heating system. It should be capable of keeping the living room, bedroom, bathroom, hallway and kitchen at a temperature of 21 degrees centigrade, approximately 70 degrees Fahrenheit, when the outside temperature is below freezing . Remember that you almost certainly will be responsible for paying the fuel bill of your own apartment and you will want to know the likely cost. Ask the warden if she can give you an idea of the size of individual bills or perhaps you might know someone already living there who could tell you. Even if the individual costs are covered by the service charge, you are still paying that and want to be assured that the system is as economical as possible.

Look for light switches level with door handles. Electrical sockets should be at least 500mm, approximately 20 inches, from the floor.

ALARM SERVICE

There must be an emergency call/ alarm system connecting each individual house to either the warden's house or to a central control. If a central control is used, there must also be a secondary control point in the warden's house.

WARDEN SERVICE

The guidelines lay down that there must be a warden service but give no information on what that service entails. You will want to ask exactly what kind of service is provided, and when, and exactly what the warden can and cannot do. You will want to know all about the costs of the wardens and any assistants. This includes items such as salary and national insurance costs, whether or not any community charge is paid for the warden, assistants and spouses and any training costs. All these items are paid for by you either directly through your service charge or indirectly through housing benefit or income tax.

OPTIONAL FACILITIES ACCORDING TO SCOTTISH OFFICE GUIDELINES

There are also a number of OPTIONAL FACILITIES that MAY be provided under the Scottish Office guidelines. You will want to think carefully about your personal situation and needs in order to judge which of them you would consider essential for your situation.

You might find that each house had been built to "wheelchair standards" which means that there is sufficient space round each fitment within the house to allow a wheelchair to manoeuvre now, even though the occupant does not use a wheelchair. This allows maximum flexibility when allocating and using houses now and in the future.

You might also find that a communal lounge is provided, with or without a small pantry or kitchen.

In a small development of up to twenty houses, you could expect to find one or two guest bedrooms for use by visitors. Larger developments could have even more. You would expect to see wash-hand basins in these rooms although they could share toilets and shower rooms. You might find that the relief warden used one of the guest bedrooms as necessary, or there could be a separate relief warden's room.

You could find a separate toilet for wheelchair users and perhaps a communal bathroom. This could have a special bath for aided bathing, a toilet, wash-hand basin and possibly a shower with grabrails at each.

If a communal laundry is provided, the washing machines and driers should be capable of prolonged, heavy use and should be big enough to cope. Recommended sizes are that a washing machine should be capable of taking a 7kg or 15lb load and a drier an 8kg or

18lb load. There should be one sink or wash basin and storage units for every 30 houses. Check that the laundry is linked to an external drying area and that there is adequate ventilation and space for ironing.

Other facilities could include a kitchen and toilet for the staff, a cleaner's cupboard on each floor, refuse bin stores, public telephones.

The standard of heating in the communal facilities should be the same as in the houses themselves, but there could be less heating in enclosed corridors and hallways.

All the communal facilities could be linked to the emergency call/alarm system.

APPENDIX 2

HELPFUL PUBLICATIONS

**FOR SALE FROM AGE CONCERN SCOTLAND,
54A FOUNTAINBRIDGE, EDINBURGH, EH3 9PT**

Your rights, a guide to money benefits for older people £ 2.50
Your taxes and savings, a guide for retired people £ 3.95
Your health in retirement £ 4.50
Calling for help, a buyer's guide to emergency alarm systems £ 2.95
Residential Care — is it for me? £ 2.95
All prices include postage and packaging

FREE ON RECEIPT OF A STAMPED ADDRESSED ENVELOPE FROM AGE CONCERN SCOTLAND

Factsheet No 1 - Help with Heating
Factsheet No 2 - Sheltered Housing for Sale
Factsheet No 8 - Moving Home - The Options
Factsheet No 12 - Raising an Income or Capital from your Home
Factsheet No 13 - Elderly Home Owners - Sources of Financial Help with Repairs
Factsheet No 16 - Income Related Benefits: Income and Capital
Factsheet No 17 - Housing Benefit & Community Charge Benefit
Factsheet No 25 - Income Support and the Social Fund.

**FOR SALE FROM SHELTER (SCOTLAND),
65 COCKBURN STREET, EDINBURGH, EH1 1BU**

Access to social housing, a survey of local authorities' and housing associations' allocation policies £ 4.50 plus 50p p&p
Rural housing in the 1990's £ 1.50 plus 50p p&p

FREE FROM SHELTER (SCOTLAND)

Stopping harassment and unlawful eviction
Warm homes and the law
Care and repair leaflet
Full publications lists are available from both Age Concern Scotland and Shelter (Scotland) on application.

FREE FROM NHBC SCOTLAND, 5 MANOR PLACE, EDINBURGH, EH3 7DH

The NHBC Sheltered Housing Code (Scotland) (draft)

APPENDIX 3

ADDRESSES

For **Care and Repair** services in Scotland contact :-

Claire Stevens	Glen Buchanan
Housing Policy and Projects Officer	The Care and Repair Initiative
Age Concern Scotland	Shelter (Scotland)
54a Fountainbridge	53 St Vincent Crescent
Edinburgh	Glasgow
EH3 9PT	G3 8NQ
Telephone 031 228 5656	Telephone 041 204 2154

Shelter Housing Aid Centres can be contacted at :-

103 Morrison St	47 Belmont St	53 St Vincent Crescent
Edinburgh	Aberdeen	Glasgow
EH3 8BX	ABI 1JS	G3 8NQ
Tel 031 229 8771	Tel 0224 645586	Tel 041 221 8995

Cruse	**Disability Scotland**
18 South Trinity	Princes House
Edinburgh	5 Shandwick Place
EH5 3PN	Edinburgh
Telephone 031 551 1511	EH2 4RG
	Telephone 031 229 8632
Scottish Federation of Housing Associations	**Citizen's Advice Scotland**
40, Castle Street North	26 George Square
Edinburgh	Edinburgh
EH2 3BN	EH8 9LG
Telephone 031 226 6777	Telephone 031 667 0156

Look in your local telephone directory for local Citizen's Advice Bureaux.

Look in your local telephone directory for local Advice Centres or Welfare Rights Offices or contact your local Social Work or Community Education Departments for their addresses.

APPENDIX 4

APPLICABLE AMOUNT LEVELS WHEN WORKING OUT YOUR HOUSING BENEFIT

BENEFIT RATES 1992/93

ADD TOGETHER EITHER -

PERSONAL ALLOWANCE FOR A SINGLE PERSON	£ 42.45
PERSONAL ALLOWANCE FOR A COUPLE	£ 66.60

PLUS ONE OF -

PENSIONER PREMIUM FOR A SINGLE PERSON	£ 14.70
PENSIONER PREMIUM FOR A COUPLE	£ 22.35
ENHANCED PENSIONER PREMIUM FOR A SINGLE PERSON	£ 16.65
ENHANCED PENSIONER PREMIUM FOR A COUPLE	£ 25.00
HIGHER PENSIONER PREMIUM FOR A SINGLE PERSON	£ 20.75
HIGHER PENSIONER PREMIUM FOR A COUPLE	£ 29.55
CARERS PREMIUM	£ 11.55

PLUS, IF YOU QUALIFY -

SEVERE DISABILITY PREMIUM FOR A SINGLE PERSON	£ 32.55
SEVERE DISABILITY PREMIUM FOR A COUPLE WHERE ONE QUALIFIES	£ 32.55
SEVERE DISABILITY PREMIUM FOR COUPLE WHERE BOTH QUALIFY	£ 65.10